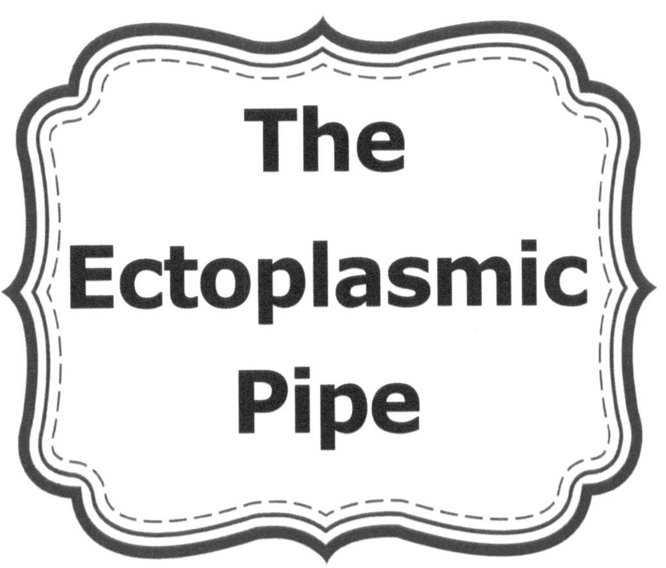

Don Schaeffer

Cyberwit.net
HIG 45 Kaushambi Kunj, Kalindipuram
Allahabad - 211011 (U.P.) India
http://www.cyberwit.net
Tel: +(91) 9415091004 +(91) (532) 2552257
E-mail: info@cyberwit.net

Printed at Repro India Limited.

to

Jim Edwards
Faith Johnston
Barbara Feller

Preface

When my artist friend and I got together, all we talked about was failure, failure of fame, failure of use.

I guess art is all about failure. Almost all art is an excerise in failure. Artists suffer endlessly for their failure to get it right and failure in life, for their abandonment and their ignorance.

The main reason for this is that there is not room for enough storage in all the world for all the art. Our basements are full. No one will accept our gifts. We have to beg or even pay to have people view our work. Storage is the main obstacle to art.

Fragment

Ectoplasm consisted of tiny numbered pieces that had to be maintained and continuously sorted into a mysterious but natural order. The bright world, brushing by, kept scrambling the parts. I always dreaded losing the inventory of parts which sat precariously in my memory. With age, as I became confused, the periods of disrepair grew. The task of finding the pieces became increasingly hard. It was so tempting to relax my lonely grip. But the question kept entering my mind, what if the ectoplasm should fail?

Filament

The body was equipped with mechanical memory. The emotion was recorded as a pattern of short wave breathlets and packets of mucous somewhere near the heart. The tears themselves were banked in the chanbers of sinus above the eyes.

As hope began, tencaiously, to return, the body would smell whiffs of sea wind and feel the bubbles rising through the thoat. The releasing of the locked clogs and the ticklish wavelets that rode the large breathing muscle were intoxicating and worth repeating.

Contents

The God Wrestler

I gave you a full plate, a life
of calm and plenty. I gave you
a world that
quenches your appetities.
That should be enough!

.

What if I have a
dull hunger in my heart?
What if I repel
peace?

.

I gave you the robust
breadth of the Earth.
That should be enough!

.

What if I sit
quietly and yearn
to stretch? What if I
harbor a bomb
of discontent?

.

I gave you
the full, rich pastiche of
human accessibility. That
should be enough!

.

What if I burn inside
with extraordinary fancies?
What if I cry?

On My Parent's 50th Wedding Anniversary

My fatherès lip
still has its Bronx street curl,
plowed over by so many
years of words.
Above his nose,
rounded by joy,
the sharp line sits,
waiting to catch the flim-flam.

My mother has the face of
someone trained in how to wait,
sliding beneath the elayers of fear and pleasure,
and a great pucker of the present crying out,
Right now! Yes!

After a Falling Tree in the Forest

Question:

If a man only found his poetry in dreams,
would he still be a poet?

Answer:

Yes.
Poetry sometimes
leaks
into life
and the people all say
"That's odd."

La La La

The little songs
that occur to me
as I do my chores
become dream songs.
I break them
and contemplate each
measure. They come from
holy memory,
a place of worship.
They are small
angels, locked into
what remains of me,
nothing but a string
of old breaths.

Making a Difference Dream

How did I get to be chairman?
That's what they all asked
And I rushed around
forgetting to
introduce myself.

.

There was no one to
take notes so I
began scribbling
logic on scraps.
They were all

.

about to leave
when I said something
rational and wrote a
line which kept them
at their desks,

.

in their cubby offices
or at the table
(I can't recall).
I just knew I'd be back.

.

I wrote lines
about water system improvement and
when I awoke
I worried where I
left the paper.

Five Minute Date

Hello Gypsy.
I'm Dave,
always 46
sideburns with

.

a touch of gray.
Do you like it?
I have a
dimple in my

cheek, left over
from my chubby days.
I know how to
smile, controlled

.

without
letting the smile
free.
I own my face

The Unwanted Offspring

When he birthed
the new baby book
that mewed and puked
in the city air
she could frighten you.

.

And the infant
pushed at her sides crying
give me room, move a little
but they refused. The senior books
sang with voices loud and clear.

.

He nursed his book
and hoped for her.
He paid for every breath she took,
crushed as she was
on little girl shelf.

.

They were fast to hide her,
mask her, *existence is a privilege* they said.
A baby book is
an imposition, not a contribution.
She strangled in a box.
It was an unattended funeral.

Strange Moses-Like Dream

I know already
don't have to wait.
Told that I can
order one to
plan in advance
but a service
brought it to me,
already done.
I saw myself
sprawled out
on the floor,
sprawled on the floor.
I tried to elaborate
putting women
in the picture
to make it erotic
as I usually do
but it ended
too soon.

Names Magnified by Dreams

Your name
is a bright spot
in my imagination,
a center of
pleasure currents
like the flow of magnets.
When I arrive at
the dull plak of morning
Something of your name
radiates from iridescent
memory. I lie
here in the night
ready for judgement.
I may as well be awake
when you won't lend me
the joy of your name.

When You Don't Answer Me

It's a special
hurt when the
distortion that brings us
into kinship at last
feels distasteful to you.
You get clean.
When I am still sullied by it,
Apparent love
grown out of
ugliness shared
cannot survive.

The Planets

Light binds the space
and time and motion are
the same. The stars are
intensified space,
the doing and the being
are the same like the spider
with the formula for webs
curled around her birth.

.

I went to the symphony
and watched the fingers
of the players, curled around
their strings and brass buttons
making feelings out of threads
of time. Just fingers as levers
for the past. The doing and
the web of being are the same.

A Poetic Apperception

It's because you
are a being of two,
that your poems
always start with
another.

.

I saw
on one of the last
warm days of summer,
how the fattened spider
emerged from her shade
and strutted
in her web.

.

and as I passed the fence
the dog barked
in units of five
bow wow
wow wow wow.

.

Is nature
always so orderly:
two and three
female and male?
It seemed a miracle.

Sci Fi Story about Murder

I am getting very strange,
spending my days
begging the buzzing-
through-the-sky
to keep me from
silence, refusing to age.
The lack of sound
is like a shadow
masking the sun.
In twilight I don't laugh.
I only fear the withdrawal
of speech, withholding
of sense, unmet standards
that compel the invisible
judges to say no.

The Erstwhile

I am a man
committed to delusion.
I congress with
ghosts. I make
projects that
tickle my vanities.
Seeming to myself
to do huge good works
with the real impact of dust.
The world
is solid and mighty.
Its gravity
pins me
to the ground
while in my mind
I fly.

Freud

1.
When you are in a strange place
you need your cell phone
and I keep losing mine
and discover hours later that it's gone.
And the woman
I came to the meeting with,
I think she's
my wife, the capable one
went off for
coffee with a friend
and I cant find her.
We are about to leave
and I don't know where
the train is. Will she come
back and I be out of reach?
On an inspiration
I beg them at the desk to find
a simple flip phone, as
familiar as my hand, but I can't
recall the brand. When the clerk gestures
to the lost and found box
hope rises. But he brings me an old
intercom instead and I explain the difference.
Is it time to leave? Will she not return?
I imagine my own bed, in the warmth of my room.
But how will I reach it?

.

.

2.
I'm heading cold into
a hollow under the sky.
Day has darkened
and night has met her,
pale, inflamed.

.

I talk like a man,
rigid, terse.
Admit nothing,
only laugh and
swing my fists.
The doors don't close
and windows leak, cold.
The vault of sleep
is two thousand miles on
the other side of torn space.
Waiting brings me deeper
into the storm
Chilled, not a place for mammals.
Only the wild fish are home.

Fast Waking-Up Prayers

When it sours
it sours hard.

The visions begin
to pour through
brain eyes and
become little
prayers, that God
slips into a cosmic
pile of quick
pleas for silence.

Dear God, they begin,
why are You sending me these
visions of happiness?

Did I Get Up?

Yes, I did rise up
and came to you
I said hello
as sunlight just

.

peeked across the trees
through the clouded window.
I narrated all this
motion by motion

.

word by word. You were
not here to see it
nor was I really.
But did I get up?

.

Did I speak to no one
in the room? I don't remember
motion or word?
I don't recall.

The Ultimate Cheat

Is there
anything wrong
with reading your own poems,
smiling through the night?
In your mind
is a concert hall
filled with love.

Drama

We saw A Doll's House
yesterday. The air was
full of needles while the
stage was dancing in
vacant fire-warmed
Christmas assumptions.

I didn't worry about
the dark although
I only prayed my joy
from the alter of my bed.
God, I said, I belong here.
I have been speaking frankly.

Self-Styled

There is no achievement
in the career of a faceless
poet. He is a poet
only in his own eyes,
clouded with wishes.

.

Each poem is merely a boast
consuming precious time
that could better be filled
with silence. Each book
crushed on the shelf
steals space from things
that really matter.

.

What would people think
if you didnt love me?
How real is love
like that ?

Why Can't They Say It Themselves?

They let the streams
speak for them
they put the feelings
in the water in the spring.
They listen
with awe to the wind
adding the rage
out of their own hearts.
The put the joy in the sun.
Joy wasn't there
before they came.
They lend life to the silent rock.

A Silent Membership

I belong to the village
of nameless fictions.
They know me.
They know me.
Whenever I appear
a little light goes on.
They whisper inside
you are here.

.

They may not
direct words my way,
and there are
no gestures but
this is my visiting
light and time.

.

We dont have
the power of sound
and most of us
don't want it.

Mr. Dreamer

I noticed how
I've slipped
out of today and tomorrow.
I've noticed that they are gone.
The nameless days are small and fast.
.

I think about the time
that has no days.
I ask where
what no one worries about
comes from,
vanishes to.

Days of Play

How do I say
that I discovered daydreams?
My mind is rich with play.
I let it go. I cavort naked,
unimpeded by impossibility.
My friends cluster about with
muzzy brains full of
driven dreams. We
permit ourselves to
to laugh and curse at nothing.

The Drama

A dozen characters
none of whom
have speaking parts,
selected from a
mystery chart,
gather themselves
in the dream,

a bowl of memories
like halloween candies,
digital, elemental,
used to make a shape,
then shift
to make another.

Ectoplasmic Pipe

A syrupy strand
extended from the ghost,
the kind I grew up fearing,
the cold stuff of germs
and life. The cooled off
product of a hot inside
locked onto my flesh,
here in the dark and silence,
like a life cable,
I come back into
invitation, voice and hope.
I don't yet
age in the dark.

Emotional Tourism

I took a trip
to victory
stripped and proud
with someone
on knees at my feet.
I watched terror and
trust in an opponent's eyes.
I vacationed in exotic
defeat and the beauties
of deep submission
under the thighs
of overwhelming strength
with hope and pride
consumed.
I travelled to these
strange lands in my
single heart.

Gravity and Ice

I fall often enough
the sky full of swarming,
circling clouds,
action massed against me.
.

Falling is the loneliest
of disasters and I
reach out for a weapon
to keep me company.
.

I call for it by name
at least I'm not alone
in those timeless instants
helpless among enemies.

Rumor at Sinai

We're told it happened.
It spun the
galaxy of tales.
They spoke it,
sending what happened
through time, the groundwork
of mystery, and we
don't know what it was.
There's talk of the bang,
dark clouds and ashes
with a deep core
of something wrapped in it.
We don't know what
the people saw that
went beyond the story
and started dreadful new chapters.

Don't worry

It is made easier
when the door comes open.
The links to ease and pleasure
are suddenly broken
the days pass with the wind
that ties your legs.
Arms can't stretch enough.
You begin begging
for the smallest pleasures.
You can organize nothing
because your hold on the world
has slipped and the earth
spins about you throwing
the ashes of what you wasted
in your eyes.

The Experience of Being Alive

When I read the poems
about the corners,
the edges, the sweet,
deep crevices of lives
beyond my telling,
I cower and hide my face
my eyes dry.
.

But when I wake up
at six-fifteen,
so loaded with
pieces of dreams,
I ask, which one
should I choose?

www.ingramcontent.com/pod-product-compliance
Lightning Source LLC
Chambersburg PA
CBHW051830130726
47987CB00003B/1480